C000067834

**A co-production between Carte bl
Theatre (London) and the Carrefour ....
City)**

Not One of These People
by Martin Crimp

Not One of These People is a creation of Carte blanche (Québec City),
produced with the support of Conseil des arts et des lettres du Québec,
Conseil des arts du Canada, Ville de Québec and Fonds Francois Gagnon.

Not One of These People was first performed at Théâtre La Bordée
(Québec City) on Wednesday 1 June 2022 as part of the Carrefour
international de théâtre, and was first performed in the Jerwood Theatre
Downstairs at the Royal Court Theatre on Thursday 3 November 2022.

Not One of These People
by Martin Crimp

CAST
Martin Crimp

Director/Designer **Christian Lapointe**
Creative Developer **Guillaume Lévesque**
Lighting Designer **Caroline Ross**
Sound Designer/Sound Engineer/Technical Director **Gabriel Filiatreault**
Dramaturg **Andréane Roy**
Assistant Designer**Julie Lévesque**
Assistant Director/Production Manager **Véronic Marticotte**
Production Consultant **Anne McDougall**

For the Royal Court, on this Production:

Stage Supervisor **TJ Chappell–Meade**
Lighting Supervisor **Max Cherry**
Stage Manager **Laura Draper**
Lead Producer **Chris James**
Sound Supervisor **David McSeveney**
Lighting Programmer **Stephen Settle**
Company Manager **Mica Taylor**
Costume Supervisor **Lucy Walshaw**

The Royal Court wish to thank the following for their help with this production: Alex Constantin

Not One of These People
by Martin Crimp

Martin Crimp (Writer/Performer)

As writer, for the Royal Court: **In the Republic of Happiness, The City, Fewer Emergencies, Advice to Iraqi Women, Face to the Wall, The Country, Attempts on Her Life, The Treatment, Getting Attention, No One Sees the Video.**

Other theatre includes: **When we have sufficiently tortured each other: 12 Variations on Samuel Richardson's Pamela (National); Men Asleep, The Rest Will Be Familiar to You from Cinema (Deutsches Schauspielhaus, Hamburg); Play House, Play with Repeats, Dealing with Clair, Definitely the Bahamas, Four Attempted Acts (Orange Tree); Cruel and Tender (Young Vic/ Vienna Festival).**

Opera includes: **Into the Little Hill, Written on Skin, Lessons in Love and Violence, (with composer George Benjamin).**

As translator, for the Royal Court: **Rhinoceros, The Chairs.**

Other translations and adaptations include: **Cyrano de Bergerac (West End/BAM); The Misanthrope, The Maids (Young Vic); Roberto Zucco (RSC The Other Place); The Triumph of Love (Almeida); The False Servant, The Seagull, Pains of Youth (National); Gross und Klein (Sydney Theatre Company/Barbican).**

As director, theatre includes: **Play House (Orange Tree).**

Awards include: **Olivier Award for Best Revival (Cyrano de Bergerac); WhatsOnStage Award for Best Revival (Cyrano de Bergerac); John Whiting Award (The Treatment); Premio Ubu (Fewer Emergencies); recipient of the 2020 Nyssen-Bansemer theatre prize.**

Laura Draper (Stage Manager)

As Stage Manager, for the Royal Court: **Glass. Kill. Bluebeard. Imp, The Cane, The Woods, The Children, Torn, Hope, Love and Information.**

As Company/Stage Manager, other theatre includes: **Jack Absolute Flies Again, Rockets and Blue Lights, Top Girls, Julie, The Deep Blue Sea (National); A Number, Girl From The North Country (Old Vic); The Comeback, The Father (West End); A Midsummer Night's Dream, Happy Days (Young Vic); Little Eyolf, Bakkhai, Ghosts (Almeida); Fathers and Sons, The Night Alive (Donmar).**

Gabriel Filiatreault (Sound Designer/Technical Director/Sound Engineer)

Theatre includes: **Constituons! (Carte blanche), When we have sufficiently tortured each other, Portrait of Restless Narcisim (Carte blanche); Maître et Marguerite (Ex Machina); Le Pouvoir (Système Kangourou); Éclipse (Marie Brassard).**

Music includes: **20 Printemps, Territoires (Le Vent du Nord); Festival Colline (Chapelle du rang 1); Dhrupad Music (Gundecha Brothers).**

Contempory Dance includes: **Tic-Tac Party + Ylem (Fila 13); Dialogue (Wei Wei Dance); Dérives (Lucie Grégoire Danse).**

Circus includes: **Hémisphère (Projet Sanctuaire); Geysers (Les 7 doigts).**

Christian Lapointe (Director/ Designer)

As director: by Martin Crimp, theatre includes: **In the Republic of Happiness (Grand Théâtre, Québec); The rest will be familiar to you from cinema (Espace GO, Montréal); When we have sufficiently tortured each other (Théâtre Prospero, Montréal).**

Symbolist plays: **Pelléas et Melisande (Théâtre du Nouveau Monde, Montréal); Limbes (Calvary, Resurrection, Purgatory) (National Art Centre of Canada, Ottawa); Axël (Théâtre Prospero, Montréal).**

Others include: **L'homme atlantique (et La maladie de la mort), Les fracophonies en Limousin, Oxygène, Carrefour International de Théâtre, C.H.S. – pour Combustion Humaine Spontanée (Official selection of Festival D'Avignon).**

As director, designer and performer: **Tout Artaud?!, Constituons!, Offending the Audience (Festival TransAmériques/Montréal).**

Christian Lapointe is the artistic director of Carte blanche, Québec City.

Guillaume Lévesque (Creative Developer)

Theatre includes: **P@ndora, Dreaming Now (with Michel Lefebvre); The Pencil Project (with Jacques Poulin-Denis, Martin Messier); Madame Louis 14 (with Lorraine Pintal).**

Concerts & events include: **Danser Joe, Red Hot Chili Peppers: The Getaway Tour, Muse: Drone Tour (Moment Factory).**

Julie Lévesque (Assistant Designer)

Theatre includes: **Cabaret, La Duchess de Langeais (Le Trident); La Paix des Femmes, Who's Afraid of Virginia Woolf? [Costume Designer] (La Bordée); Six Degrés, Crepuscule chapitre 3 – Vents et Marées (Cirque Flip Fabrique); Où tu vas quand tu dors en marchant…? (Carrefour international de théâtre).**

Véronic Marticotte (Assistant Director/Production Manager)

With Christian Lapointe, theatre includes: **Titre(s) de travail, We are shining forever à la recherche de l'entrée du royaume des morts.**

Other collaborations includes: **Jouvence, Parc Optimiste (with Étienne La Frenière); H+ (with Emile Beauchemin); L'Incroyable et Ineffaçable Histoire de Sainte-Dignité-de-l'Avenir (with Odile Gagné-Roy & Steven-Lee Potvin); Les Muses Orphelines (with Amélie Bergeron); Scénarios pour sortie de crise (with Olivier Lépine); Alors voilà, Fin septembre début janvier (with Eudore Belzile).**

Caroline Ross (Lighting Designer)

Theatre includes: **Les Chaises, Tout Ce Que Tombe, La Famille Se Crée En Copulant, Les Reines (with Frédéric Dupois); Les Pieds Des Anges, Une Vie Pour Deux, La Cantate Intérieure (with Alice Ronfard); Madame De Sade (with Genest); Mycologie, Nicole (with Stéphane Crête); Un Jour ou L'Autre (with Brigitte Poupart); Océan (with Pol Pelletier).**

International events & exhibitions include: **The Quadrennial of Scenography (Prague); Star Wars Identities, Danser Joe (Moment Factory); Being Augustine (Société des Musées du Québec).**

Awards include: **Best Lighting Award 2018 (Les Chaises); FÉLIX for Best Lighting Designer, 2015 (ADISQ); Grand Prix d'Excellence (Being Augustine); Show of the Year 2011 (The Threepenny Opera).**

Andréane Roy (Dramaturg)

With Christian Lapointe, theatre includes: **Pelléas et Mélisande, (Théâtre du Nouveau Monde, Montréal); The rest will be familiar to you from cinema (Espace GO, Montréal); When we have sufficiently tortured each other (Théâtre Prospero, Montréal).**

Others includes: **Sportriarcat (with Claire Renaud); Hidden Paradise (with Alix Dfresne & Marc Béland); Parce que la nuit, Sang (with Brigitte Haentjens); Et quand vient le silence (Grand Surface); L'école des femmes, Zoé (with Olivier Choiniére).**

Andréanne also collaborates with Centre des Auteurs Dramatiques, the National Theatre School of Canada, as well as the publications Jeu and Aparté.

THE ROYAL COURT THEATRE

The Royal Court Theatre is the writers' theatre. It is a leading force in world theatre for energetically cultivating writers – undiscovered, emerging and established.

Through the writers, the Royal Court is at the forefront of creating restless, alert, provocative theatre about now. We open our doors to the unheard voices and free thinkers that, through their writing, change our way of seeing.

Over 120,000 people visit the Royal Court in Sloane Square, London, each year and many thousands more see our work elsewhere through transfers to the West End and New York, UK and international tours, digital platforms, our residencies across London, and our site-specific work. Through all our work we strive to inspire audiences and influence future writers with radical thinking and provocative discussion.

The Royal Court's extensive development activity encompasses a diverse range of writers and artists and includes an ongoing programme of writers' attachments, readings, workshops and playwriting groups. Twenty years of the International Department's pioneering work around the world means the Royal Court has relationships with writers on every continent.

Since 1956 we have commissioned and produced hundreds of writers, from John Osborne to Jasmine Lee-Jones. Royal Court plays from every decade are now performed on stage and taught in classrooms and universities across the globe.

We're now working to the future and are committed to becoming carbon net zero and ensuring we are a just, equitable, transparent and ethical cultural space - from our anti-oppression work, to our relationship with freelancers, to credible climate pledges.

It is because of this commitment to the writer and our future that we believe there is no more important theatre in the world than the Royal Court.

Supported using public funding by
ARTS COUNCIL ENGLAND

Carte blanche produces theatre with scenic forms rooted in the prism of the visual, performative and multidisciplinary arts. Its mandate is to encourage theatres to take risks by creating innovative co-production projects.

Since 1979 Carte blanche has created some 50 new productions, a significant number in partnership with the largest producing companies in Canada, as well as with international producers from the French-speaking world.

Christian Lapointe has been the artistic director of Carte blanche since 2013.

Being both a festival and a producer, the Carrefour international de théâtre is a meeting point for artists, arts professionals and the public. We work in close collaboration with the theatre community by being a complement and a partner in making theatre and creation thrive.

Focussed on theatre, the Carrefour's choices are surfing the flow of today's trends in contemporary theatre. Its program can be distinguished by the quality, eclecticism and diversity of the experiences offered to the public. The aesthetics and the subjects, where circus, dance and art often interact, and the great diversity of locations where the plays are presented are other prominent qualities of the Carrefour.

CALQ
Conseil
des arts
et des lettres
du Québec

COMING UP AT THE ROYAL COURT

Fri 18 Nov–Sat 17 Dec
BAGHDADDY
By **Jasmine Naziha Jones**
BAGHDADDY has been generously supported by a lead gift from Charles Holloway.
It is a co-production with SISTER.

Thu 19 Jan–Sat 25 Feb
SOUND OF THE UNDERGROUND
Written by **Travis Alabanza**, co-created by **Debbie Hannan**

Thu 09 Feb–Sat 11 Mar
GRACELAND
By **Ava Wong Davies**
Graceland is a co-production with SISTER.

Tue 14 Mar–Sat 29 Apr
BLACK SUPERHERO
By **Danny Lee Wynter**

ASSISTED PERFORMANCES

Captioned Performances

Captioned performances are accessible for people who are D/deaf, deafened & hard of hearing, as well as being suitable for people for whom English is not a first language.

Baghdaddy: Wed 7 Dec at 7.30pm & Thu 15 Dec at 2.30pm

Sound of the Underground: 8, 15 Feb 7.30pm

Graceland: 3, 10 March 7.45pm

BLACK SUPERHERO: 12, 19 April 7.30pm, 27 April 2.30pm

BSL-interpreted Performances

BSL-interpreted performances, delivered by an interpreter, give a sign interpretation of the text spoken and/or sung by artists in the onstage production.

Sound of the Underground: 22 Feb 7.30pm

ASSISTED PERFORMANCES

Audio-described Performances

Audio-described performances are accessible for people who are blind or partially sighted. They are preceded by a touch tour which allows patrons access to elements of theatre design including set and costume.

Baghdaddy: Sat 17 Dec at 2.30pm (Touch Tour at 1pm)

Sound of the Underground: 25 Feb 2.30pm with TT at 1pm

BLACK SUPERHERO: 29 April 2.30pm with TT at 1pm

ASSISTED PERFORMANCES

Performances in a Relaxed Environment

Relaxed Environment performances are suitable for those who may benefit from a more relaxed environment.

During these performances:

– There is a relaxed attitude to noise in the auditorium; you are welcome to respond to the show in whatever way feels natural
– You can enter and exit the auditorium when needed
– We will help you find the best seats for your experience
– House lights may remain raised slightly
– Loud noises may be reduced

Baghdaddy: Sat 10 Dec at 2.30pm

Sound of the Underground: 18 Feb 2.30pm

Graceland: 11 March 3pm

BLACK SUPERHERO: 22 April 2.30pm

If you would like to talk to us about your access requirements, please contact our Box Office at (0)20 7565 5000 or boxoffice@royalcourttheatre.com
The Royal Court Visual Story is available on our website. Story and Sensory synopses are available on the show pages via the Whats On tab of the website shortly after Press Night.

THE ROYAL COURT THEATRE

The Royal Court Theatre relies on the support we receive from individuals, trusts and corporate partners to help us to achieve our mission of supporting, nurturing and empowering writers at every stage of their careers. Through our writers, we are at the forefront of creating restless, alert, provocative theatre that reflects the world in which we live and our mission is more important than ever in today's world.

Our supporters are part of the essential fabric that enables us to keep our finger on the pulse – they give us the freedom to take bigger and bolder risks, challenge the status quo and create world-class theatre that affects and disrupts the theatre ecology. It is through this vital support that the Royal Court remains the writers' theatre and that we can continue to seek out, develop and nurture new voices both on and off our stages.

Thank you to all who support the Royal Court. We really can't do it without you.

To find out more about supporting the Royal Court please get in touch with the Development Team at support@royalcourttheatre.com, call 020 7565 5030 or visit royalcourttheatre.com/support-us

ROYAL

BAR & KITCHEN

The Royal Court's Bar & Kitchen aims to create a welcoming and inspiring environment with a style and ethos that reflects the work we put on stage.

Offering expertly crafted cocktails alongside an extensive selection of craft gins and beers, wine and soft drinks, our vibrant basement bar provides a sanctuary in the middle of Sloane Square. By day a perfect spot for meetings or quiet reflection and by night atmospheric meeting spaces for cast, crew, audiences and the general public.

All profits go directly to supporting the work of the Royal Court theatre, cultivating and supporting writers – undiscovered, emerging and established.

For more information, visit
royalcourttheatre.com/bar

HIRES & EVENTS

The Royal Court is available to hire for celebrations, rehearsals, meetings, filming, ceremonies and much more. Our two theatre spaces can be hired for conferences and showcases, and the building is a unique venue for bespoke events and receptions.

For more information, visit
royalcourttheatre.com/events

Sloane Square London, SW1W 8AS Sloane Square Victoria Station
 royalcourt theroyalcourttheatre royalcourttheatre

COURT

SUPPORT THE COURT AND BE A PART OF OUR FUTURE.

Every penny raised goes directly towards producing bold new writing for our stages, cultivating and supporting writers in the UK and around the world, and inspiring the next generation of theatre-makers.

You can make a one-off donation by text:

Text **Support 5** to 70560 to donate £5
Text **Support 10** to 70560 to donate £10
Text **Support 20** to 70560 to donate £20

Texts cost the donation amount plus one standard message. UK networks only.

To find out more about the different ways in which you can get involved, visit our website: royalcourttheatre.com/support-us

The English Stage Company at the Royal Court Theatre is a registered charity (No.231242)

Not One of These People

Martin Crimp was born in 1956. His play *Attempts on Her Life* (1997) established his international reputation. His other work for theatre includes *When We Have Sufficiently Tortured Each Other*, *Men Asleep*, *The Rest Will Be Familiar to You from Cinema*, *In the Republic of Happiness*, *Play House*, *The City*, *Fewer Emergencies*, *Cruel and Tender*, *The Country*, *The Treatment*, *Getting Attention*, *No One Sees the Video*, *Play with Repeats*, *Dealing with Clair* and *Definitely the Bahamas*. He is also the author of three texts, *Into the Little Hill*, *Written on Skin* and *Lessons in Love and Violence*, for operas by George Benjamin. His many translations of French plays include works by Genet, Ionesco, Koltès, Marivaux and Molière. *Writing for Nothing*, a collection of fiction, short plays and texts for opera, was published by Faber & Faber in 2019.

MARTIN CRIMP

Not One of These People

faber

First published in 2022
by Faber and Faber Limited
74–77 Great Russell Street
London WC1B 3DA

Typeset by Brighton Gray
Printed and bound in the UK by CPI Group (Ltd), Croydon CR0 4YY

A CIP record for this book
is available from the British Library

ISBN 978-0-571-38143-2

Not One of These People was first performed at Théâtre La Bordée, Québec City, on 1 June 2022 (in English by Martin Crimp) and 2 June 2022 (in French by Christian Lapointe).

The play was first performed in London on 3 November 2022 in the Jerwood Theatre Downstairs at the Royal Court Theatre.

Text and Performance Martin Crimp
Director and Designer Christian Lapointe
Creative Developer Guillaume Lévesque – o/1 Hub numérique
Lighting Designer Caroline Ross
Sound Designer, Technical Director and Sound Engineer
    Gabriel Filiatreault
Dramaturg Andréane Roy
Understudy Sylvio Arriola
Assistant Designer Julie Lévesque
Assistant Director and Production Manager
    Véronic Marticotte
Production Consultant Anne McDougall

For the Royal Court:
Stage Supervisor TJ Chappell-Meade
Lighting Supervisor Max Cherry
Stage Manager Laura Draper
Lead Producer Chris James
Sound Supervisor David McSeveney
Lighting Programmer Stephen Settle
Company Manager Mica Taylor
Costume Supervisor Lucy Walshaw

A creation of Carte blanche (Québec City).

A co-production of Carte blanche, the Royal Court Theatre (London) and the Carrefour international de théâtre (Québec City).

NOT ONE OF THESE PEOPLE

1   I went into that meeting fully expecting to be fired.
    I said, look, I've come to this meeting fully expecting
    to be fired. And I was right, they fired me.

2   I'd got up to about page ten and was feeling pretty
    pleased with myself. After all, I'd only been learning
    Japanese for, what? – four or five months now? So
    I showed it to my girlfriend – who is Japanese –
    obviously – why I'm learning – and I asked her about
    some of the words which I hadn't understood. So she
    says to me: you do realise this is a rubbish book?
    I said, what d'you mean it's a rubbish book? She says,
    it's a rubbish book, it isn't literature, it's trash. Not
    'well done, you've started to read in Japanese'. Okay,
    I said, in that case I'll read some literature. Then Miki
    tells me literature's too difficult – plus some of it's
    actually written in Chinese.

3   I was a few pages in and I had to stop reading. The way
    he describes women, the way he talks about women,
    the way he treats women as objects, the things he
    makes them say, the thoughts he attributes to women
    which no woman would ever have, the sexualised gaze,
    the distaste for women of middle age, I couldn't go on
    with it. In fact I've stopped reading male authors, I've
    just stopped, I've completely had enough of it.

4   I don't know how many times I've already told you this.

5   I don't know what she said to you, but whatever it
    was it wasn't true.

6	I've never seen the sky looking so blue.

7	I'm not convinced by any of it – never have been.

8	There was a very good reason to kill him with a hammer.

9	When I went in for the assessment I said, look, are you medically qualified? They just didn't care that I couldn't breathe.

10	I was very surprised when she explained to me that I was part of the patriarchy.

11	I can't resist antique coffee pots.

12	I don't think I'm going deaf particularly, I think what's happening is people are mumbling a lot, especially kids, kids mumble, they've stopped articulating, know what I mean? Because I can still hear the tiniest little sounds – fly bangs into a window, toaster pops up. Or someone's got those things plugged into their ears – tss tss tss tss – drives me completely crazy. Or you're having a conversation and they're tapping away on a computer. No it's not me going deaf, it's the way people've started to talk now, it's not even the English language, know what I mean? – just mumble mumble this and mumble mumble that. So I'll say to some girl who's tap tap tapping away: articulate, sweetheart, don't just mumble, can't hear you. And sometimes they point to this sign says respect in the workplace or whatever. So I say I do respect you in the workplace, sweetheart, but I'm not deaf, and I'm not stupid, I just need you to say it a bit more clearly. I mean if I can hear a fly banging into a window.

13   He said to me, you can say what you like – I said, oh
      can I? Can I really say what I like? I don't believe
      you. And he goes: well it's just the two of us, sure you
      can say it, sure you can. So I say: you're not going to
      like it. And he's like: what? You're not going to like it,
      you're not going to like me saying what I like, that's
      all. So he says: is it about the squirrel? Well alarm
      bells started ringing then and I say, what are you
      talking about: squirrel? So he's just grinning and
      going, come on, say it, you can say it, you can say
      whatever you like, you can say whatever is on your
      mind – squirrel, horse, just say it. And I'm really
      angry now – not just about the squirrel, but about
      this whole assumption not just that I'll say what I like
      if it's him I can say it to, but that *he already knows*
      what I'd say if I was given the opportunity to say it.
      So I say to him: this is nothing to do with squirrel,
      you've no idea what I'd say if I said it, don't kid
      yourself, you've as much chance of knowing what I'd
      say if I said it as you have of wintering in the
      Bahamas. And he's like wintering in the Bahamas –
      what? So I'm like: you heard. So he says: is this what
      you'd say if you could say what you like? – is this
      it? – are you saying it? And I'm like: you will never
      ever know what I'd say if I said what I liked – and
      what's more I will probably never say it – not to you,
      and not to anyone – not to anyone ever.

14   Turns out I was the reason she was thinking of killing
      herself.

15   Turns out he'd been lying to me for the past thirty-five
      years.

16   Turns out I have extra-sensory perception and I can
      hear what people are thinking.

17   It was impossible for me to be honest with my
      mother – or with my father. I did try and be honest
      with my mother's sister but she's got her own
      problems with her daughter's stepchildren.

18   When he started calling himself a cis-man, I could see
      what he was trying to do, but it meant our
      relationship was over.

19   The weird thing was was I changed at Frankfurt, then
      changed again at Frankfurt. I still don't understand
      how I could've changed at Frankfurt twice.

20   Of course it was when he apologised I felt maximum
      contempt for him – I mean actually physically sick.

21   I tried to explain that I couldn't live on that amount
      of money: in fact nobody could. And in the end I was
      getting even less.

22   If queer's the new normal, I found myself thinking,
      then what's the point of my queerness? I've been
      upset about this for quite a few days now.

23   I had to look up mise en abyme in the dictionary.

24   You could see from the way she was around me that
      she loved me. She definitely definitely was in love
      with me. She couldn't hide it. This happens to me all
      the time.

25   I like all those 1970s colours like orange.

26   Don't get me started on the right-wing press.

27   You know what he calls Virginia Woolf? Suicide
      Bitch!! I mean I was shocked.

28   We're both totally polyamorous – sure, sure, she's more into it than I am. But yeah – polyamorous – both of us – totally.

29   Someone is going to have to explain Foucault to me.

30   I went into the meeting fully expecting to be fired. I said, look, I've come to this meeting fully expecting to be fired. They said: explain that, why should we fire you? So I explained everything that had happened – not just about the Post-it notes, but everything. And that's when they fired me.

31   I like trees, I like nature, I like to be outside, I'm not laughing, I mean it.

32   I'm not saying kill her, it's not actually a death threat, it's a measure of my depth of feeling – she can't just attack our community in the way that she has and give offence in the way that she has and not expect death threats but I'm not saying that, I'm not saying kill her, that's a deliberate misreading. The fact you're even challenging me about this shows how out of touch you are.

33   I'm one of those people where nothing works out for me – ever.

34   I'm one of those people who leads a charmed life: everything always works out for me.

35   I'm one of those people who I read about someone moaning that nothing works out for them and I've got no sympathy for them at all. They should just get over it.

36   I'm not one of those people who I hear about
      someone who's really successful and at peace with
      themselves and I want to kill them.

37   I really don't like lemons. It's the zest, it's the zest.

38   I'm not one of these people who goes on a retreat and
      then when I come back from the retreat I bang on
      endlessly about how much the retreat has changed
      me. I'd say the people who say the retreat has
      changed them are the people who haven't changed at
      all – know what I mean? I find myself at dinner
      sitting next to someone who's banging on about how
      much the retreat has changed them and I'm thinking
      to myself: 'arsehole – you haven't changed one
      fucking iota – you've always been like this.' Okay so
      it's uncharitable of me, I'm just telling it like it is.

39   Any man over forty wearing a leather jacket and
      immediately alarm bells start ringing.

40   It's a perfectly friendly dog but you just have to be
      watchful. It's a great dog, family dog, great with kids,
      all I'm saying is be watchful – same as you would in
      any home or family situation.

41   I transitioned for the high heels, for the glamour, for
      the bathroom camaraderie and bikini tops, for looking
      pretty in the mirror, feeling hot. So now is someone
      trying to tell me these things are wrong? – that I
      shouldn't desire what I desire? Because you asked me
      what I think and what I think is that what we need to
      do is shift the whole meaning of the word feminism.

42   It's really hard to be a white person now. I mean I'm
      not saying it's ever been easy – but right now? – in
      the climate as it is now? – yea, yea, pretty difficult.

43   I need a man to be a man, I want to be fucked – can I
      say that? I don't want him to keep asking 'Is this
      alright? Is that alright?' – I need him to know and
      just do it.

44   I respect what you're trying to say and sure we're
      comfortably off but we've worked pretty hard for
      that. There's trees, there's grass, there's space for the
      kids, holidays, we like a nice bottle of wine once in a
      while, who doesn't! And sure, there's the so-called
      second home, but it's hardly a palace, some cottage in
      a field, to tell you the truth we just inherited it, dirt
      track, no proper heating, more of a pain than
      anything else, you couldn't spend winter there.
      Because okay there's us – by which I mean the vast
      majority – and then there's your three Lamborghini
      brigade, there's your conspicuous wealth brigade, the
      private jets, the private islands – that's where the real
      money is and that's where I agree with you that it's
      politically indefensible.

45   You know there's this thing where a white person
      says to you so what did you think of *Moonlight* – or
      what's your take on, I don't know, *Invisible Man*.
      And the fact is they're not asking 'me' what 'I' think –
      they're just seeing me as a generic 'person of colour'.
      They're the kind of people who want a Tin Man's
      perspective on *The Wizard of Oz* – 'we need to
      include Tin Men in the conversation' et cetera et
      cetera. They don't realise that if I'm anyone at all I'm
      Dorothy.

46   Say I see a little girl now, and she's at the edge of a
      cliff or something, and her parents are nowhere in
      sight, what am I supposed to do? – go up to her?
      Especially if she's pretty. I'm just saying.

47   Say I'm taking my dog for a walk and there's this sign
No Dogs. I mean what sort of a message is that
giving not just to people like me but to the
population at large? No Dogs. That is an insult.

48   Say I was a vegetarian – which I am – and someone
puts in front of me a piece of meat – which they do, I
mean they frequently do – then I'm in a very difficult
position. Because often it's a friend that's put that meat
there, you know? Well I say friend – but whoa! – hang
on a minute! – is someone who puts meat on your
plate really a friend? Because they just keep doing it, I
mean giving me meat – when surely they know. I mean
by now they must know that I find a piece of meat –
any meat – on a plate like that revolting. I'm going to
have to recalibrate a lot of my friendships.

49   Say I could have my life all over again, well I
wouldn't've got married – at least not to him – I'd
still've had kids – although not those ones, obviously.
I wouldn't've worked: total waste of time – I'd've
found someone who could keep me, I don't have a
problem with that. I'd have these really nice
girlfriends where we went out every lunchtime for
cocktails. I'd probably have my first drink around
nine a.m. – probably vodka in a glass of orange juice.
At first I'd hide it from my kids – the new ones,
I mean, who'd be really sweet – but then I'd stop
caring whether they saw me or not. I'd have this cool
silk dressing gown, Japanese type thing, kimono, and
I'd sit in a really lovely kitchen drinking and putting
on weight. My husband – I'm not talking about him,
I'm talking about the new one – would be really into
looking after me. He'd be like, 'I think we've got a bit
of an alcohol problem here, let's get you some help.'
But I'd say: no, it's not a problem, Jared – or
whatever his name was – Romesh. I'd say: it's not a

problem, Romesh, you gorgeous man, I'm just so
incredibly happy. Is it weird to be thinking like this?

50   Say I was thirteen again I would definitely not
     masturbate.

51   Say I could have a special power – know what?
     I don't want one. I'm happy to be an ordinary human
     being – because ordinary human beings already have
     amazing powers of love, of empathy, of creativity and
     self-fulfilment. Plus can already destroy things at a
     distance. I don't really understand the question.

52   Say private corporations were harvesting data about
     my movements and my private conversations – so
     what?

53   It's true that I'm pretty successful now and that some
     people pay attention to me in a way which is both
     flattering and scary. Is it because I'm a woman that
     I have this feeling? – what's it called? – this impostor
     feeling? Or is it simply (which I think is more likely)
     simply that this cultural thing was never part of my
     childhood or family or anything. Say I'm at one of
     these parties, we're in a garden, there's cypress trees,
     lots of little snacks on plates. And there in the garden
     are, you know, film-makers and dancers, money
     people and opera producers plus one or two very
     famous faces and the snacks on plates keep
     circulating. It's not that I feel I don't belong – sure
     I belong – I was invited! So no, it's nothing to do with
     being an impostor – aren't we all impostors of one
     kind or another? – no, it's about what's inside and
     what's outside. Are those cypress trees and snacks
     inside of me or outside of me? Where's the light? Out
     there in the garden? – or inside my mind? And
     voices – sure, they're all around me – but once I hear

17

them, aren't they a part of me? Can people be inside you? And yes, ha-ha, I don't mean fucking, I mean where are those voices really located?

54   I wrote a whole book about the colour blue then realised I'd left out Campingaz containers.

55   I've had to adjust to the fact that my children can inhale smoke and die and nobody actually cares.

56   It's not something I wanted, or desired, or hinted at, or ever thought about, or read about, or prepared for, or had fantasies about, subconsciously wished for or dressed for. I didn't invite it, or conjure it, or try and imagine it, or try not to imagine it, or welcome it, or encourage it, or lay the ground for it, devise a scenario for it, set the atmosphere, create an atmosphere, a mood, provoke, or set the tone for it. And yet it happened. It's a miracle.

57   I've noticed that the arguments around surrogacy can get very very emotional, and that there are people who can't accept the monetisation of women's bodies and who believe that ovaries, say, or the uterus, have some kind of magical value and should not be priced. I've also noticed that it's privileged white women who are skilled at making these arguments against the black or brown women who stand to gain economically from entering the reproductive market.

58   I've noticed the men in my rifle club getting very defensive about issues of consent.

59   I've started to notice family members asking me if I'd like a glass of water or a nice chocolate biscuit. Okay, I'm dying, but that doesn't make me stupid.

60   What I immediately noticed was one: his hair was
        white – and two: he looked like a twat.

61   Crack! Bang! Oh my god the sense of power! Have
        you never fired a weapon? You need to try it. Because
        I used to think: this is not for me – then it's breathe
        slowly out and crack! bang! – I'm totally addicted.

62   I notice myself about to say things which I suddenly
        realise it's better not to say. So my mind swivels, it
        swivels really fast now. And everyone else's minds are
        swivelling too. There's this whole dance of not-saying
        where everyone steps back and swivels.

63   I've lost count of the number of times I've been told
        'I don't see race, I'm colour-blind'. Then they smile at
        me as if they're expecting what? – to be rewarded?

64   I've lost count of the number of times I get called
        second generation immigrant. Because excuse me?
        but if I'm 'second generation' – and thanks so much
        for your validation – how can I be an immigrant?

65   I've lost count of the number of times I wake up and
        I'm really disturbed. You don't mind me saying what it
        is? Because my partner's sick of it – the dream, I mean –
        he just doesn't want to know. And I get that, but I
        mean this dream is very powerful, it's a powerful
        dream – and it's true that it's about him, and maybe
        about some aspect of him he'd rather not know about
        or hear about and of course I do scream out, I scream
        out every time it happens – but still. I get out of bed –
        this is in the dream – I'm out of bed, I don't know why,
        I'm standing by it and there's a sound. Well the sound
        is coming from under the bed, it's a kind of scraping,
        and so I can find out what the scraping is, I get down
        on the floor on my hands and knees and look under

the bed. Well under it's a kind of Barbie doll, same size, no clothes on, and it's moving. The doll-thing's on its back with its legs apart – which you can't of course do with an actual Barbie – so that's already weird – and it's trying to sit up – which a Barbie can do – but this one's pushing with its hands, it's like a little person, got its hands flat down and its fingers spread apart and it's trying to push itself up. Now the thing is that it's trying to talk. It's kind of muttering and you know it wants to say something but because of all the pushing it can't speak, just goes on pushing and pushing at the floor which is what makes the scraping noise. So I push my head further under the bed so I can talk to it and hear what it's trying to say – because now what I realise is that it must be terribly important, and maybe the Barbie-thing is one of my children and it's come back and it's trying to tell me something. But that's when my partner grabs me from behind. He grabs me from behind, and tries to lift me off the ground. Maybe he thinks that's funny, and maybe it *is* funny – but I bang my head as he swings me up, and that's when I start screaming.

66   I can hear when something's inauthentic – a voice that's been – whatever – stolen or appropriated – it's like I've got perfect pitch that way.

67   I can hear her saying, we're so thrilled to have a voice here to represent your community – and of course I'm smiling and being super-thrilled back – but in my mind I'm going: Community? What the *fuck*?

68   I can hear people on other planets – it's not their voices, it's the cutlery: it's when they clatter with their forks and spoons. On Venus, for example, they have limestone tables. Don't look at me like that – I'm joking. I said I'm joking.

69   I'm watching it because I've heard it's anti-Semitic.

70   I couldn't watch it because of the violence.

71   I watched it but it made me very angry.

72   I had broadband issues and was unable to watch it.

73   I was bored from beginning to end but perhaps that was the point of it?

74   I wouldn't watch that as a matter of principle.

75   Amazing. Brave – violent – sexy. For a man like myself it's just thrilling to see women take control of the narrative.

76   I went into that meeting fully expecting to be fired. I said, look I've come to this meeting fully expecting to be fired. They seemed a tiny bit confused, they said, explain that, why should we fire you? So I explained everything that had happened – not just about the Post-it notes, but everything. I told them about the broken glass, and that if they searched my home they'd find a number of highly volatile reagents. They said, what are you talking about, search your home? what are you talking about, reagents? I said: know something – you've never valued me, not as an employee, and not as a human being. I get up in the dark and I leave my kids to make their own breakfast just so I can come here and wipe down your surfaces. Admit it: you think I'm scum. And that's when they fired me.

77   If you think you know what it's like to be me you are seriously deluded.

78   That's when I ask myself if I've even a right to speak.

79   People like me've been silenced for years and years
      and years.

80   It's true – sure – that his books are narcissistic, but
      I recognise myself in that.

81   So he's on his fourth prosecco and suddenly comes
      out with how I can't appreciate what it's like to be
      him, there's stuff going on in his mind – dark stuff –
      childhood and shit – stuff going on in his mind I've
      just no access to. So I go, what is it I don't have
      access to exactly? – is it the bottomless self-pity? –
      or maybe the taste for pert fifteen-year-olds? Well
      that makes him laugh – and he goes: 'Don't say pert,
      it's sexist.' So I tell him women can't be sexist, only
      men can – lying, obviously. And he's like, bollocks
      there's plenty of women bitching about other women,
      starts in the playground and it never stops – plus
      gender's just constructed, didn't you know? So I'm:
      well shame when they constructed you, babes, they
      left the nuts off.

82   I'm not one of these people who can't take a joke. I
      can. I really can. No – I mean it – I absolutely can.

83   I'm sorry: I don't watch television.

84   I'm sorry: I didn't realise you were in the queue.

85   I'm sorry: you can't claim my experience as your
      own.

86   I'm sorry: but Y chromosome means you're a man.

87   I'm sorry: but I'll write what the fuck I like.

88 I'm terribly sorry, but I think you're sitting in my seat.

89 I'm sorry, but I had exactly the same background –
I recognise those streets, I recognise those estates,
I know what it's like to be frightened to wet the bed
because you're having to share it with two of your
sisters – but look at me now: I'm in government and
I did not receive a single handout.

90 I'm sorry, but if you talk that way you will receive
death threats. You will receive them. I'm not
supporting it, I'm just saying it's inevitable.

91 I'm sorry, but by endlessly stressing the vulnerability
of young women you're recreating a Pre-Raphaelite
world of russet-haired victims.

92 I'm sorry, but you've come to the wrong building.
This is the embassy, you need the consulate.

93 A man cannot understand the experience of rape. I'm
sorry, but it's a fact.

94 I wake up each morning and I'm quite happy. I can't
help myself: it's my temperament. Even if it's cold and
dark I'm still smiling to myself. I know! Some people
hate me! They think it's strange to be so happy all the
time. Maybe it is strange! I can't help that! I've got
this little jug that was my mum's – meant to be from
Jamaica – don't think it is though, think it came from
Debenhams. So that's what I make my coffee in – nice
to have it in a jug so you can pour it. Mum was a
character – always so proud of our light skin.
Shocking to think about it now, shocking to even say
it out loud. Because I do think things've got better –
not perfect, obviously – and there are people who
would strongly disagree – strongly strongly disagree –

and I respect that. But like I say, it's my temperament, I'm an optimist – even in the cold and dark! Five a.m. you just have your own thoughts.

95   My parents were therapists.

96   I couldn't mentally rotate the cubes that ought to have shown me how intelligent I was.

97   Dice? What's that about? No, I have no idea what's opposite the number three. Sorry, I think that is a fucking stupid question.

98   I turned towards her in the car and kissed her.

99   Yes, I'm responsible for screening the fertilised eggs and then implanting them. Your question?

100   I'd got to about page ten and I was having my usual thoughts, i.e. you've got to stop this now, you can't go on with this, come on, just stop – the usual business of self-criticism meets self-pity, the usual nausea, the hovering angels of self-censorship looking over my shoulder and so on, plus now the whole dread of speaking: is it something new this dread of speaking? So anyway I've got to about page ten, the usual point for destroying everything – but now let's say I don't, let's say there's a change of heart here, a decision not to destroy: a thought that I've been pulled up high enough by the motorised plane to be detached from it now and glide. The cable drops away. The motorised plane returns to the airfield. Let's say I'm alone now in the transparent cockpit. That line of trees shows where my village ends. Beyond, they're setting up a fairground. That tiny cone – look – must be the helter-skelter, and that tooth-edged yellow wheel the roof of a horse-roundabout. Dip the wing and, as the horizon

tilts, a greenhouse flashes back light. Graves in miniature shore up the miniature stone-built church – and so on and so on – as I begin to wonder if the whole thing might not just possibly be endless.

101   I poisoned my next-door neighbour's cat. It was surprisingly easy.

102   I was especially warm and friendly about my brother-in-law coming to visit with his family since I knew that during the dates he was proposing I had arranged to be out of the country.

103   I dropped my partner's toothbrush into the toilet and lied to her about how it'd got wet.

104   I stole my daughter's boyfriend. I feel bad about it, but I did say he was too old for her.

105   I got up at six thirty a.m., I dressed for work, out through the door by seven, not back until maybe eight in the evening – even later sometimes. What did I do all day? Well – I'd start in a coffee shop – then there are parks, cinemas, art galleries, department stores. I kept it up for about six months, then there was a problem with the washing machine, the kitchen flooded, she couldn't get me on my mobile, so she called me at work. Exactly. I came home that evening and there was a bit of a reckoning.

106   There was an immediate spark with me and Karin but it was a year or so before anything happened. One reason of course was her commitment to the cause – which she was not just passionate about, it was her life. The other reason is that she didn't find it easy to . . . what's the word? – give herself, yes give herself to another human being. But in the end, she

did: we married, we had Benjamin, we had Klara, we
led an ostensibly normal family life. Yes looking back
I had obviously started to lose my bearings
somewhat. But I enjoyed being a father – I believe
I was a good one, and a good husband to Karin –
strange as it may seem to say that now. My job –
sure – hundred per cent correct – was to infiltrate the
organisation, collect data about the membership,
facilitate surveillance – and in that I was successful.
I admit there were shortcomings on the personal side
of things.

107   To get him to have sex with me I pretended I was
eighteen.

108   My boss knows that I saw some of what went on
between him and Katya, and that I happen to know
Katya was not happy about it. Well I can't say I
particularly like Katya, so even if she knew that I'd
seen and wanted me as some kind of witness, I
wouldn't get involved with Katya in that way – I'm
sorry – just not. I'm not exactly blackmailing my
boss, and I'm not exactly 'betraying' Katya – but I am
now aware that there's a much stronger chance of me
getting her position and of Katya being let go.
Women like Katya do tend to exploit how they look
and use it to manipulate men – so while I'm not
condoning my boss – that kind of behaviour in the
workplace is so out of order – I'm just not prepared
to stick my neck out in this particular instance. I
suspect there'll soon be a round of people reapplying
for their jobs and that could well be an opportunity
for Katya to leave. My boss is a little uncomfortable
around me now – smiling a lot, using my name a lot,
asking me almost every day how my kids are – it's
creepy, but I do think it's a positive sign. I've also
reminded HR that, given the current climate, Katya

may not find it so easy to renew her visa this time round. Is that the kind of thing you mean?

109   I never pulled the wings off flies, but I did burn ants.

110   We had a boy in our class called Christopher Smale. Christopher Smale had dirty brown hair. He often got into trouble for being stupid. The teacher would make him come up to the front and he'd tell us about the new stupid thing Christopher Smale had done. I knew it was cruel – but that's why it made me laugh.

111   I used to deliberately break the point of my pencil so I could use one of the electric sharpening machines.

112   I got moved to a different desk because Heather Hazlewood kept trying to touch my penis.

113   I used to pretend to my brothers that I was falling down the toilet. I also made them be horses so I could whip them.

114   I went up behind this girl who'd been bullying me in the playground and pushed her over.

115   I did this thing on a job just outside of Oxford where I deliberately let a roof slate drop four storeys onto a busy pavement. Done it twice now, actually.

116   I did this thing where I used to line up a little speck on the car window with people in the street and imagine it was a machine gun and kill them.

117   I did this thing – don't know if you've ever done this? – where I found someone's phone on a train and instead of trying to identify the owner I started

calling all her contacts and telling them she'd been involved in a serious accident.

118   I do this thing – don't ask me why – where I say my name's Anastasia and pretend I've got Russian parents.

119   Anything at all? Okay. Well I do this thing – not very often – but do do this thing where I know someone's a vegetarian so I deliberately serve them meat.

120   I do this thing – obvious really – where I don't join in a conversation till I've listened for long enough to work out what everyone else thinks. Oh, and if I get introduced to new people I instantly forget their names unless I find them sexually attractive.

121   Say I turn up at a client's house and first thing they say to me's not 'How d'you like your coffee?' but 'We're hoping there won't be a lot of dust' – well what I do is this thing where I disconnect the boiler and don't come back for another six days.

122   I do this thing where I leave my bike in the entrance hall when the regulations which govern my tenancy explicitly forbid it. Why? Because it's much more convenient. Oh and I also tip food waste straight into the communal bins, which is apparently why there's a rat problem.

123   I do this thing where say a man is looking at me on a train and he's being inappropriate, so what I do is just say in a really loud voice: 'Rapist.' Why? You're kidding me.

124   I did this thing where a minibus was approaching a checkpoint and I totally destroyed it. Women. Children. Everyone. Why? Those were my rules of engagement.

125 I didn't do that thing you're supposed to do where you acknowledge what your sources are and thank everyone. The other thing I didn't do was provide a safe space for my respondents or recognise that soliciting their stories might cause them psychological damage.

126 I can't do that thing where one of the girls I was at school with has a baby and I'm supposed to go into ecstasies. I'm just thinking: life over.

127 Me? I won't do that thing where at the airport they make you put your toothpaste in a little plastic bag.

128 I did this thing – must've been twenty years ago? – is that too long? – no? Okay, well I did this thing where for two or three days I completely disappeared. It was from a Wednesday evening to a Saturday morning – as I say – twenty years ago. I'd been drinking with my friend Michaela and the last thing she saw was me going out the door with a man called Colin – who was some sort of artist. Well I can see what you're thinking, but the fact is is, is that according to Michaela – who I do still occasionally keep in touch with – but according to her, this Colin came back after just five minutes with a stupid smile on his face because he had been so shocked. He said that out in the street, where we'd gone outside to smoke, I'd started to speak a foreign language. He said he didn't recognise what the language was, but that I seemed totally serious and not like I was making it up. The reason he was so shocked – well this is what Michaela told me Colin said – was that while I was speaking this other language I started to get aggressive. He said I seemed frustrated at not being understood and began to lash out. He said I'd punched him in the face – and Michaela confirms that his mouth was in fact bleeding. Well they both

came out into the street to look for me, but I'd gone: that was the Wednesday night. So on Saturday morning I wake up and the phone's ringing and it's Michaela and Michaela's like, where've you been? – we've been worried sick – can I come round? So Michaela's in my kitchen, and that's when I start to realise I can't remember the last couple of days. She's telling me what Colin said to her about speaking another language and punching him – and I can't remember that either. She says: d'you want me to come with you to the police? And I say: police? – you're joking – what's stuff I can't remember got to do with the police? Well, Michaela says, it's your choice. She's got this bunch of flowers and she's started to open my kitchen cupboards looking for a vase – which I'm sure that she means well, but is just very slightly frightening, opening all my cupboard doors like that. She's also upset me with this story about the other language: I don't speak other languages, never have, don't need to. You asked me for a 'confession' – and I suppose what I'm confessing is not that there are two days of my life looks like I was careless enough to lose – it's that, although I still occasionally see her, I don't trust Michaela – not her real name, obviously. I don't trust Michaela (a) because she opened my cupboard doors, and (b) because she put words into my mouth via this man Colin which I can't even understand, let alone contest. I mean, no big deal, I don't lose sleep over it, I'm not 'traumatised'. You probably won't even want to use this.

129 I lost control and mounted the pavement.

130 I said the first thing that came into my head.

131 I lied when I told him I couldn't get pregnant.

132   I asked for her private number – ostensibly for work.

133   For some time now I've been carrying around with me
       a squeezy-bottle filled with concentrated sulphuric acid.

134   I go on writing even though it's mediocre.

135   I smile without showing my teeth.

136   I put a green bottle into the slot marked Clear Glass.

137   I stamped on a snail.

138   I conspired with my wife to cheat my brother-in-law
       of his inheritance. Whenever the phone rings now,
       I won't pick up.

139   I plundered other people's work for stories. I
       appropriated their voices. I ventriloquised characters
       from diverse cultures. I wrote voyeuristically about
       rape and passed off disturbing acts of violence as
       entertainment. I cross-dressed and flirted with gender-
       fluidity but only as a means to ram home
       heteronormative conclusions. I also invented a
       Caribbean island.

140   I set a book in America without having been there.
       I claimed the experience of being an insect as my own.

141   An African-American – as I would now be styled –
       I egregiously wrote the story of a gay white man in
       Paris.

142   A woman of what I hesitate to style the upper middle
       class, I showed an egregious lack of empathy for the
       working-class women whose labour gave both me
       and my female characters the leisure time to think.

143   A gay white man in Paris – as I might now be styled, given that, as time passes, we must put on the disguise of the cultures that come after us and attend, wearing our most brilliant smiles, the parties that future generations have thrown apparently in our honour, but in reality where our skulking presence would not after one or two hours be especially missed – a gay white man in Paris – as I believe I might now be styled – I made the mistake of staging a fictional heterosexual obsession in which I presented the narrator's female victim as a zero-dimensional mash-up of sexual perversity and deceit.

144   I made the mistake of opening a tin can at the wrong end which means the label is upside down when you try to read it.

145   I made the mistake of going ahead with testing the reactor when the workers on that shift didn't have the skills to cope.

146   I made the mistake of trusting him. I made the mistake of each time he hit me thinking it was my fault. Loving him in the first place: that was my mistake. Lot of mistakes.

147   I made the mistake of inviting my parents for Christmas.

148   I made the mistake of coming here and listening to this shit.

149   I made the mistake of doing this ever-so-humble all-my-fault business when I should've just told her to fuck right off.

150   I made the absolutely classic mistake of reading my partner's emails.

151   Do I make mistakes? – not really – mistakes, mistakes, let me think. Can't say there's anything particular springs to mind. Okay – well – there was a time when I – anything, right? – well a time when I was living in Germany, and I was seeing this guy, and his parents – not him, obviously – but his parents had been close, if that's the word, to Ulrike Meinhof. And anyway, one day he takes me to this exhibition by some famous German painter – don't remember his name now – man, obviously – and turns out it's paintings of Meinhof. It's these black-and-white pictures of Ulrike Meinhof dead, plus some of the others – what's that other one called? – Varder? Baader? – something like that. Well I hated it, I was really really upset, and I made the mistake of saying to Thomas, Thomas this is just so fucked up, I can't stay here, I have to go out – thinking Thomas would follow me and come outside and see how I was. But Thomas just stayed there, he just stayed there in the gallery talking to his friends. And that was it: I quit Frankfurt and I refused to have anything more to do with him. Did I make a mistake? Not sure. Also can I just ask what is the point of this?

152   I'd already made the mistake of giving him my number. Then I made the mistake of asking him why he wouldn't wear a condom. Turned out he couldn't get hard enough to use it.

153   I basked in the sun while my kids were screaming.

154   I persuaded myself I was a genius.

155 I told myself that what I could feel could not be a lump – even though it was a lump and I could feel it.

156 I told myself that the more people I managed to offend, the more I was showing my independence of thought.

157 I told myself that if I adjusted the Scrabble score in my favour it was reasonable because right from the start I'd had such crap letters.

158 I let myself think that there was something going on in the kitchen, when there wasn't. I also convinced myself that my thoughts weren't private – were being harvested by corporations and displayed publicly on enormous screens – in Singapore, mostly. This turned out not to be true. I do still notice that some people are able to read my thoughts – but I put that down to basic mind-reading. Do I still think there's something going on in my kitchen? – Of course there isn't – what makes you say that?

159 Me and my sister managed to persuade ourselves mum would be happier living in a care home.

160 I managed to persuade myself he was in love with me and not just using me for sex.

161 Light's made of particles, right? Well I managed to persuade myself not only that I could see the particles, but that I could actually collect them – you know: if I held this box at a certain angle then snapped the lid shut? I do in fact think that there are particles of light inside the box, but obviously if I take the lid off they'll escape, that's why I'm not going to risk it. It's a general problem, really. We all know the world's made of these very small particles, but everyone's in denial about it.

162 I actually found that when I did sex work I had a more honest relationship with men and they on the whole usually treated me better than they did in so-called real life. In many ways it's much easier when the financial side of things is totally explicit.

163 I can't stand mirrors. The person I see in the mirror is not me. The body I see in the mirror is not my body.

164 I can't stand dogs. Sorry. If I see a dog or a dog comes up to me in a public place, I will say to the owner, 'Can you please put your dog on a – f-word – lead.' I've just got no time for it – don't care how 'loyal' or companionable they're supposed to be. Plus when they lick their own – to use the polite expression – genitals? – what's that all about? I recognise their strengths when it comes to drugs or explosives – I grit my teeth and I work alongside them – but can't say I'm thrilled about it. There's also dogs now can tell you've got cancer? Doesn't surprise me in the least – there you are with your hair falling out feeding it fillet steak.

165 I'm sorry but what I cannot stand is people with children. Train door opens, suddenly there they all are with their kids and their kids' buggies and kid-size backpacks – and I'm thinking: oh shit, school holidays. I mean let's be quite clear about this: it's not the kids' fault – but the arrogance of the parents, that's what gets me. It's the entitlement. It's the 'yes we know life on earth is unsustainable but we're somehow exceptional' – know what I mean? Then they're actually standing on the seats with their shoes on and no one says anything.

166 I'd prefer not to have to say this, but I can't stand being inside my own head. Or rather: it would be okay if the other person wasn't there, looking on,

trying to control me. What's he like? Well it's not always a he, sometimes it's a she – there's no reason women can't be predatory and controlling! But one thing they do have in common is they're wearing a silver cowboy hat. I mean I completely understand it's not possible. I'm fully aware that a human being – like any animal – is 'just' an electrochemical machine. There is no 'Cartesian theatre'. There's nobody inside me watching, just as there's no 'me' inside me to be watched. But when they hear me say that, all they do is smile. They know they're there. They know there's lots of them in cowboy hats and I'm outnumbered.

167   I wasn't grateful for the clothes I was given. They didn't fit well and I thought they aged me. At home you choose your own clothes – obviously – from what you can afford. So opening a plastic bag and just having to wear whatever's inside it, things that other people've been wearing and given away, I found that humiliating. Not that I'd ever say it. I failed to be grateful – yes.

168   I failed to be grateful, I failed to acknowledge my privilege, I failed to acknowledge it wasn't about me.

169   I failed to adjust the clocks. I missed my flight. I failed to make the connection and that is most probably why I'm now divorced.

170   I failed to be coherent.

171   I failed to stop at a red light – easily done – but on this occasion I unfortunately killed someone.

172   I failed to see things from the perspective of other people.

173   Failure is not a word I am happy to use, I find it demeaning – but I do fail to see the humour in some of the things some people seem to find funny.

174   What's that thing Kafka says? – 'The outside world's too small and clear-cut to contain everything that a person has room for inside'? Yes and it's true I've spent most of my life attracted to what's on the outside: 'issues', politics – when I'd originally had dreams of all the magic rooms, all the shimmering landscapes I was going to create. Made money, sure – but as an artist, you're so right to point out I completely failed.

175   I just could not keep my signature inside the box.

176   Oh my god the thing I always fail to do is wash my hands before touching it.

177   I failed to kill myself. Really embarrassing. That's one hotel I always steer well clear of.

178   I walked out without paying.

179   I overtook on the inside.

180   I forced my whole family to go on a camping holiday.

181   I taught swear words to a five-year-old. I smashed a plate.

182   I smashed a plate. I dressed provocatively as a woman: I minced.

183   I minced, I faked my CV, I stole, I stereotyped.

184 I sucked everything in, I spat everything out, I made the mistake of saying women enjoy sex more than men do: for that I was made blind.

185 I was made blind for what I'd said, I banged into the wall, I left dirty marks, I got irritated when people asked do you need help crossing the road, I shouted at my kids, I pushed a whole pencil into an electric sharpener till it was just a stub, hung my head in shame but was just faking it.

186 I faked shame, I faked guilt, I failed to re-enchant the world, when I walked through a country lane I slashed the tops off flowers.

187 I shouted at my kids, I said I'd started to smoke again when the fact was I'd never stopped, I claimed I'd been a war photographer: it wasn't true.

188 I said I'd suffered, I said I had been traumatised: none of it was true, I made it all up.

189 I made stuff up, I invented shit, I checked my whole family into a hotel I couldn't afford, none of it was true.

190 I 'acted black' in front of my lighter-skinned cousin's friends, I claimed to know what a bat thinks, I refused to tick boxes about ethnicity just so as white folks could feel they were listening, I sulked in my tent.

191 I sulked in my tent, I minced.

192 I minced, I faked, I stole, I stereotyped, I sucked, I spat, I fucked up, I failed, I blundered, I withheld, I rubbished, I belittled, I turned a blind eye, I parodied,

I offended, I frustrated, I coveted, I danced badly, I made the mistake of growing old, I spoke over, I bullied, I smacked, I lashed out, I drank, I gambled, I audibly unwrapped a sweet, I eyed up, I broke in, I invaded, I undermined, I mis-sold, I manipulated, I mis-gendered, I totally failed to read the room, I flirted, I creamed off, I shut out, I misappropriated, I misheard, I misspoke, I didn't sufficiently mourn, I got shirty, I went on using a blunt knife, I couldn't stop, I shouted at my kids.

193 I shouted at my kids. I said: 'Mummy has had enough.' I said: 'I'm counting to ten and if you haven't stopped, Mummy is walking out of that door and she's not coming back. D'you understand what that means?' I smashed a plate. I won the Nobel Prize for literature but wouldn't go to Stockholm to accept it.

194 I refused to go to Stockholm, I refused to go to Damascus.

195 I sulked, I avoided the battlefield.

196 I changed overnight: I was unrecognisable.

197 I found all my friends so compromised – all getting 'married', all of them having babies. And I'm like: 'Excuse me? Whatever happened to queer?' I tailgated, I bitched.

198 I tailgated, I bitched, I overate, I overthought, I released particulates into the atmosphere.

199 I released particulates, I bitched, I compromised, I deceived myself, I said I'd water my neighbour's pot plants but when they came back from holiday their plants were all dead.

200 I bitched about my boss, I hacked into company emails and filled the communal coffee machine with broken glass. I worked out how to make a bomb and started to collect in small quantities the reagents I would need to make one. Every morning I stuck to their screens Post-it notes telling them in a foreign language exactly what I thought of them all. That's why I went into that meeting fully expecting to be fired. I said, look, I've come to this meeting fully expecting to be fired. And I was right, they fired me.

201 I just opened my son's computer and there it was: explicit sex. I challenged him about it. I said to him: this is explicit sex. I was so hurt.

202 So there we are at the funeral and turns out that all of my cousin's friends are fascists and racists. I'm not kidding you.

203 So I'm like 'what's so funny?' And she's like 'this is exactly the same room I stayed in with my ex. We broke the bed.'

204 I just didn't see her. She hit the bonnet, hit the windscreen, then must've flipped over the roof and down onto the road. I'd braked of course – but by then it had all already happened. She was just not looking.

205 I didn't mean the glass to break, but I did know I was really really angry with my sister.

206 Turns out I'd been buried under – what did they say? – exactly: five hundred metric tonnes of snow.

207 The bullet went through his left eye and took the back part of his skull off. I've no idea how he found

that gun. I'd told him time and time again to stay out of Mummy's bedroom.

208   I must've been about thirty-five? – I'd begun to drink quite heavily by then, which my mum was quite down on, quite judgemental about it actually – which is when she comes out with 'Fact is, you were an accident, sweetheart.'

209   So this bus goes off the road – somewhere in Spain I think it is – goes right off the road and down this mountainside. There's all the kiddies in it – and their teachers and whatever – parents – it's a school trip basically – and what he says is: Sure, that is really sad, but it isn't tragic. And I'm thinking: You arsehole.

210   You could see the fire lighting up the whole sky orange. I was one of the first ones there – it was like a disaster movie – flashing lights and smoke – I had a suit on but I knew enough about radiation to know a suit like that was next to useless. I was pretty sick, but somehow I survived when some of my colleagues died – and of course in the end we did finally seal the thing with concrete. But the thought of it, the thought of that mass, that volume, that temperature, the thought of it burning and burning its way down into the earth, through the rock, through the aquifers, maybe endlessly – the thought of that material endlessly on fire – sometimes I can't sleep, even now.

211   And I'm like, oh my god! it's gone completely green!

212   Really it was just the tiniest cut, it was just here – I was cutting onions and the knife slipped – just here, but about a centimetre and it wouldn't stop. It was completely clean, and not so deep, but just would not

stop bleeding. So I go over to the tap and already I've
managed to get blood down my shirt – great streaks
of it – and I get it under the tap and turn the tap on,
which helps because it's cold, so I can see where the
skin is flapping open and I'm thinking to myself that
doesn't cold water reduce the bleeding? – freeze it or
something? – only what seems to be happening is that
the water is kind of encouraging the blood, the
opposite of what I'd hoped, so there's a thread of
watery blood now running down into the sink,
fascinating in its way but not the remedy I'd imagined
plus I am starting to think now how much blood can
a person actually lose? Well this is when the frying
pan bursts into flame, because the thing is, is I'd
turned the gas on knowing I could chop the onions in
exactly the time it took to get the oil hot – I like to
plan ahead that way – so the pan is not just smoking,
there are flames, quite frightening really, and I know it
is essential not to pour water into burning oil, not that
I can remember why, I don't do science, I'm more of
an intuitive kind of person, but even though I know
it's wrong about the water I can't see how else to put
the fire out plus I've already got the tap on for the
blood. So anyway I grab the handle – which is steel –
well, chromium-plated, but still steel – and of course
this metal handle is incredibly hot and I immediately
drop it and the burning oil goes everywhere. And sure
sure sure, I can see objectively how stupid I must look,
screaming like that, dropping the burning pan, blood
all down me, but personally I don't find it very funny.
And I'm sorry if that disappoints people – but my
burns were quite severe. I've been told that the issue is
probably that the knife I use to cut vegetables isn't
sharp enough.

213   Obviously it had not been my intention to sleep with
      my own mother.

214 I'd never intended to get pregnant.

215 I just wanted to get her off me. Then she tripped and her head banged into the wall. Tripped – tripped – that's right – I've already told you this.

216 Thing is, someone like me, I made my own opportunities, I wasn't just handed them on a plate, had to make them. Because I'm sorry but I look at people like this – people who are not contributing to society – and what it is is, is they're just incapable of making opportunities for themselves. Genetic? Could be. But the fact is, nothing in this world happens by chance. And that's why they're dealing drugs and getting themselves shot.

217 I remember this because it involves my mother – I was still little, must've been seven or eight? – and anyway we're on a train and this man starts to talk to her – he's like a man with a briefcase – and he opens the briefcase and he gets some document out and asks her to read it. So she takes a look at it – must be the title page for a report or something – and smiles in a way that I can now see was scare-quotes feminine and slightly deferential – and he says: see anything strange about it? And mum goes: no. So he says: well read it out. So mum reads it out and it's something like ANNUAL REPORT OF THE INSTITUTE OF ELECTRICAL ENGINEERS. And she's still not getting it. So the man goes: don't you see – they've left the T out of electrical – and we've just had printed twenty-five thousand copies. And I don't think either of us knows what this really means – is it funny – or is it something really bad? I remember my mum smiling, but without opening her mouth. All women wore lipstick in those days.

43

218   So I looked in my outbox and I had sent it to
EVERYONE – including the photographs.

219   I opened the door and there they were, kissing.

220   I knelt in the grass and that's when I saw my ring.

221   Turned out I'd married my brother.

222   Turned out my parents had selected me to be deaf.

223   I knew that the one thing I must not do was shatter
the Chinese vase.

224   Then there's the pilot welcoming us to Oslo – so I
turn to the woman next to me and we're both like:
Oslo? Isn't this the flight to Frankfurt?

225   I had created a whole world – and of course you're
sceptical, of course you are – but I swear to you I'd
created a whole world. There were trees, there was
light, I'd invented animals. There were funny little
doors you could go through, and once you were
through, there were either sequences of magic rooms,
or outdoor sequences: tracts of land, seascapes, high-
rise blocks, whole sequences of intolerable desert or of
rose gardens. And sure, there were people in them, that
was the thing I was proudest of. I invented them, I set
them in motion. Look through any of the tiny doors
and there they were, getting on with their lives as if
they were completely real. Because I'd devised this
world of mine so none of them could see me looking.
Sure, they suspected something – after all, I'd made
them clever! – and they looked for me all over – in the
deserts and so on, or maybe they'd get it into their
heads to smash a magic room up with an axe,
expecting to find me that way. I can see you don't

believe me, very few people do, and I still don't know how I managed to delete it. Strangely I'm less bothered by the fact that this world of mine has gone – and I mean gone, I mean wiped out irretrievably – than by the fact that nobody sitting around this table – intelligent as you all so obviously are – seems to believe that someone like me could ever have invented it.

226 Fiction: men. Drama: men. Poetry: surprise, surprise – all men. Okay, so 'One throw of the dice will never abolish chance' – profound – whatever. But that's for a man. What chance did women get to hang out in Paris and write poems? It's like Degas and those women in the tubs washing themselves. Sorry: creepy.

227 So it's a man picks up, and this man goes: 'Maria's phone' – and I'm like what the fuck Maria's phone? – then the penny drops: I've called my ex. Oh fuck, oh fuck, I've accidentally called my ex – and here is Mister Wax-My-Balls-Please Tai-Chi Man-Who-Understands-Me Personal I-Have-An-Infinity-Pool Shit-Face Trainer going 'Maria's phone. Who is this?'

228 I found another woman's earring in our bed.

229 I discovered it had radioactive properties.

230 I realised that the volume of my body was exactly that of the displaced water.

231 The door comes open and it's him and he is completely tongue-tied – all this: I'm so sorry, sorry, I'd no idea. You'd think he'd never seen a woman in the bath before. So I'm: don't be embarrassed, just close the door. And he thinks I mean go *out*. I have to literally say to him: come back – and now please close the door.

232   Me? Well there is something I do on the motorway which is I close my eyes and start very slowly counting. Sorry? Sure I can tell you – the most I've got up to is five – two if I've got the kids with me. Well of course when I'm driving, otherwise what's the point?

233   If they hadn't kicked me off the flight with this sorry we're overbooked and we need to prioritise families bullshit, I'd be one of those people where they're still looking for body parts.

234   If I'd been able to read Italian I'd never've met my husband.

235   If she hadn't discovered my diary, we might still be friends.

236   I'd still be getting up in the dark to basically electrocute poultry, if I hadn't won thirty-five million euros.

237   If my aunt – who was only sixteen then – had appeared just one minute earlier at the window of our apartment in Schützenstrasse, our whole family would've been arrested and killed, meaning I wouldn't be talking to you now.

238   If she'd bothered to lock the bathroom door I'd still be happily married.

239   I think we have to be realistic about this. Twin studies provide invaluable information about genetics and causality, and I think we have to recognise – obviously with enormous caveats – that much of this so-called Nazi data is actually pretty reliable.

240   I look at a butterfly's wing and I think – random mutations! – so much beauty!

241   I just happened to look up and she was staring.

242   I was staring into space and he just happened to look up.

243   I'd gone back to get my pencil – which turned out not to be there – and that's when I happened to see the two of them staring at each other.

244   My personal opinion? I'd say human beings have a one-in-two chance of surviving the century. I'm quite cool about that. What's so special about being human? – 'human exceptionalism' and blah blah blah. It's not as if organisms won't survive – just look at trees – look at the billions of insects – or the what's it called – the something something shark? I'm totally with Plato: when we die we go back to the place we were at before we were born – it's not really an issue. It wasn't such a bad place to be, was it.

245   My personal opinion? Is that fatalism is racist. Is that determinism is the prosecution of the colonial project under another name. Is that pessimism is the metaphysical aperitif of the white and privileged, consumed at sunset on the rotting verandas of their institutions. Must I name them? Very well then. Banks, the judiciary, the universities, cinema, departments of government, social media, all technology, publishing, theatres, the police. I could go on.

246   They said it's a very rare form of cancer. I said, well thank you, knowing that makes me feel so much better.

247　So much has happened to me by chance: falling into a career – meeting my lovely wife – buying property at a fortuitous moment. Even two of our children – and I know the twins won't mind me saying this – weren't entirely planned! So I don't really appreciate this accusation of privilege when so much in my life has happened purely at random.

248　Well you know me, I'm not much of a one for housework, I do the basics, but if it's say hoovering, I never use the attachments, the little brush-thing, or the whatever it's called – crevice-nozzle? – I really don't see the point of them, which is why of course the stuff down the back of the sofa, crumbs and so on, tends to remain there. And for some reason I was poking my hand down, feeling some of these crumbs, and what I found was a coin. I fished it out and it wasn't till next morning in the daylight that I thought, well that's a bit strange. So I showed it to Ruthie – Ruthie's my sister – and Ruthie says where the hell did you find this? I said, what d'you mean? She said, well look at it, it's old, you should get it valued. I said, get it valued, don't take the piss. She said, but look at the funny shape, it's all pebbly, and there's a man on it with a bow and arrow, you should see a numismatist. I said, see a what? She said, there's something about this coin, trust me, you should go to the British Museum. So I'm in the British Museum and the numismatist there – Samira – Samira says to me, have you any idea what we're looking at? And I say, no Samira, please enlighten me. So Samira tells me it's gold, weighs about eight grams, and is approximately two and a half thousand years old. The man with the bow is Darius the First, King of the Persians until his death in 486 BCE, and whose empire at its peak extended as far as the Indus Valley and included parts of Ethiopia and Egypt. This coin, she said, for which Darius set high standards of purity –

getting on, if I remember correctly, for ninety-five per cent gold – is particularly rare, since after the Persians' defeat by Alexander maybe two centuries later, the majority were melted down. You're probably aware, Samira said, passing me a jeweller's loupe so I could take a good look at the details of Darius' pleated gold tunic and the prongs of his funny little crown, probably aware of the passage in Herodotus where Darius argues for monarchy and, predictably, against both oligarchy and democracy – which he denigrates as rule by the rabble. And of course you'll remember how after deploying so much so-called reason in their political debate, they then come up with the totally bonkers idea that whoever's horse neighs first next morning when the sun comes up will be appointed king.

249 If I hadn't been brought up in a council house I might think it was normal to be middle class.

250 If I hadn't been born I might've been happier.

251 If he hadn't gone down on me I might not've noticed his bald patch.

252 I'd still be alive today if I hadn't been black.

253 If I hadn't run back inside out of the rain, slipped on the tiles, banged my head on the steps, chipped a tooth, smashed my phone, bounced off the Christmas tree, hit a child's buggy, twisted my right ankle and actually started to wet myself, I might never've got so interested in Quantum Theory.

254 If I hadn't run back inside out of the rain, slipped on the tiles, banged my head on the steps, chipped one tooth, knocked out another, smashed my phone, bounced off the Christmas tree, hit the child's buggy,

scratched my face on a bike pedal, covered myself in grease, ripped my silk trousers, twisted my right ankle, bit my own tongue and actually started to wet myself, I might not that same evening have criticised my boyfriend's choice of Japanese reading material as strongly as I in fact did.

255 If I'd had an umbrella with me when it started to rain, I'd never've run back inside, skidded across the wet tiles, chipped a tooth, smashed my phone (which I had luckily backed up), hit the child's buggy which they have been repeatedly told not to leave in the communal areas, or bitten my own tongue, I'd never've had this thing just before losing consciousness where a voice inside my head went: 'While nobody has a right to be desired, and nobody can tell another person who they should or should not desire without falling into an authoritarian trap, it is nevertheless the case that who is and who is not desired is a political question.' It's made me a lot more cautious – obviously.

256 She said I'd a one-in-a-hundred-thousand chance of getting a woman pregnant. I said, give us a break, love, I'm not that fucking ugly. No sense of humour some of these doctors.

257 Turns out the guy next door to me was in the same tsunami I was.

258 Turns out the chiropractor who has moved into the basement flat next door and is definitely – *definitely* – paying over the odds for it has exactly the same name as me. I'm envisaging all kinds of confusion, and I can flag this up right now: any letters end up here that are in fact for her will go straight into my bin.

259 Turns out this guy had found my phone? So he gets
into it – I don't know how – goes through my contacts
and calls Marianne. So Marianne picks up, Marianne
thinking it's me of course – don't know why he
chooses Marianne, but he does – so she picks up, and
there's *Benjamin*, which is the French way of saying it,
on the other end. So what happens now? Do they
work out some way of getting my phone back to me?
No. Oh no no no. What happens next is they organise
to meet. And this *Benjamin* turns out to be quite hot.
That's right: she's hit the jackpot. So they go back to
his and do not *emerge* for three whole days. So that's
three whole days, can you believe this, that I am
without my phone. And I'm like: excuse me,
Marianne, but you used to be a feminist.

260 Exxon Valdez? Deepwater Horizon? I've read the
reports and these are not quote unquote 'accidents',
these are the entirely foreseeable consequence of
unregulated global capitalism.

261 I beg to differ. I am not stateless by chance. My
statelessness is the entirely foreseeable consequence of
this country's anti-Muslim rhetoric and misogyny.

262 It can't be a coincidence that whenever I leave my
house there's a blue van parked opposite.

263 Me? Well I lived in a tiny little house with my
parents, and in the tiny little house next door was an
old lady: Mrs Horton. Well Mrs Horton died, and for
some reason we went into her house, which we'd
never been into when she was alive. The hallway was
very narrow because there was a piano in it, and the
piano stool was the kind that opened and had music
inside. Some of the music was already doing that
thing old paper does where it thins out and crumbles,

but a lot of it was intact. So I get it all back to my house – must've been about ten – and that's how I discovered the Mozart Sonatas – and the forty-eight Preludes and Fugues.

264 Me? Well okay, let me think. I'm just thinking. One moment. Still thinking. Excuse me. Takes me a bit longer to think now than it used to! But yes, there is something, and that is that I always tell my students about Francis Bacon throwing the paint. He's having this quite sardonic exchange with David Sylvester and Sylvester asks him if he throws it with a brush and Bacon says no, he just squeezes it into his hand and chucks it. Why? Because he wants to disrupt – his word, not mine – disrupt this thing – painting – that he can in fact do with ease. And anyway, when I tell my students this, they're quite excited. It starts a whole conversation about what an artist does or does not intend – which inevitably brings us on to Kant – and I think that's pretty amazing, discussing Kant with twenty-somethings on a Wednesday afternoon. Because I've got colleagues my age and older who got frightened of the kids and just gave up. They'd say to me teaching's a minefield – the gender and identity stuff's just too explosive. Then they'd mysteriously add: 'But of course you are protected.' And I'm thinking to myself – HIV-AIDS, spat at in the street for kissing another man, and don't even get me started about Uganda – sure I'm protected.

265 Me? Well one thing I just don't get is socks in a drawer. Say you take out a red sock, then have to work out what your chances are the next sock will be red too so you have a pair. I mean (a) does anyone actually care? and (b) who is it keeps their socks in a drawer like that?

266 The prize was a goldfish and I so so wanted one.
Each fish was in a little plastic bag.

267 I said to her no I am not predictable, what d'you
mean, I've done all kinds of things, we both have, I've
been spontaneous, I bought you that dress, I got you
the sexy pants, I took you to see that admittedly
awful play, got you drunk for the first time on gin,
there was the weekend in Minsk, there was the totally
spontaneous upgrade on the flight to Athens, we had
sex in the toilet, that wasn't exactly planned! – or are
you thinking it was? Because what exactly are you
accusing me of? What is it exactly about me you
think you can predict?

268 I don't know if you're familiar with the film
Blow-Up? Antonioni? 1966 at a rough guess? Well,
there's a character in it played by Terence Stamp –
Terence Stamp – pretty sure it's Terence Stamp –
Terence Stamp – I believe it's Terence Stamp –
and Terence Stamp – unless it's somebody else –
could be somebody else – but unless I'm very much
mistaken, Terence Stamp – who is a photographer –
is in his darkroom – and he's enlarging these
photographs he took outside in a park. He notices
something odd in one of the photographs, so he
makes bigger and bigger enlargements and he's
pinning them up to dry – this being the Swinging
Sixties and photography's all analogue. Then, when
he turns the lights on, he sees that what he's captured
completely by chance is this man in the bushes who's
been shot dead. No, it was David Hemmings. Terence
Stamp is Pasolini's *Theorem*. 1968. Eastmancolor.

269 I said, well what is it exactly? What am I looking at?
They said, well somehow you've managed to inhale a
drawing pin.

270 I said, history of twins, what d'you mean? Then they showed us the scan. Oh my god!

271 I said to him, look, here is your wife's heart, and this, look, is the projectile. Can you see how close the projectile is to your wife's heart? He said, is this some kind of lecture, are you trying to lecture me? I said, no, I'm just letting you see how lucky your wife has been, given the projectile's proximity to her heart.

272 There's people at work who are knee-jerk anti-advertising. They say 'if it's free, then you're the product' – like that's some earth-shattering fact rather than dreary pub-goer's cliché. Thing is, I prefer to be targeted – if something pops up about Ancient Mesopotamia or special deals in film-photography, then I find that interesting – much more interesting than random stuff about celebrities' bikinis and their 'cheeky antics in Mumbai'. I wish they'd stop droning on about algorithms.

273 Me? Well something I like to do is imagine I've no free-will. In fact it's not very difficult because according to my mum and dad I've always been quite passive.

274 Me? Well I've heard of the bell curve, I've heard of so-called Normal Distribution. But I do think we have to question this use of the word normal – because there are many many people who are quite rightly offended by it.

275 I brush my teeth, I give my armpits a really good scrub. If I'm going on a date I don't like to leave anything to chance!

276 I'm not one of those people who avoids risks. I'm just not.

277 I'm not one of those people who says they're comfortable with risk, then the moment you get them naked, pepper-spray them and release the dogs they start whining for their mummies.

278 I'm not one of these people who questions statistics – questions statistics – sorry, it's quite hard to say that, I'll try it again. Not one of these people who questions statistics.

279 I'm not one of these people who takes risks with spaghetti.

280 I'm not one of these people who looks up into the night sky and deduces from the clarity and exact mechanism of the stars or indeed from the overwhelming scent of jasmine the existence of an all-powerful creator.

281 I'm not one of these people who think women are more likely to be anxious or depressed.

282 I'm not one of these people who think men are more able to mentally rotate cubes.

283 I'm not one of these people who think when the bombing starts it's safer to stay out in the street.

284 You probably won't believe this because you're still feeling emotional, but I'm not one of those people who opened fire indiscriminately. You cannot blame me for the death of your child.

285 I'm not one of those people who have rituals they
have to go through before they leave the house so
their children won't be (for example) crushed on the
motorway – like making sure my antique coffee pot is
in the exact centre of the hall table.

286 If I hadn't had kids I might've been one of those
people whose academic theorising about the right to
have children in a world whose growing population
is 'morally unsustainable' is queasily close to the
worldview of the nineteenth-century geneticists I
assume they despise.

287 I'm not one of those ever-so-clever people who's
decided there's no free-will. Doesn't that amount to
saying that all the choices we believe we make in life
are meaningless?

288 I'm not one of those people who would take a risk
with a peanut.

289 I'm not one of those people who travels by yacht to
Monaco simply to place a bet.

290 I'm not one of these half-baked priests who sees God
as 'more of a metaphor'.

291 I'm not one of these compulsive gamblers. I do know
when to stop.

292 I'm not one of these people who'd experiment on
non-human animals – exposing their brains and so
on – just to reduce the so-called risk to humans.

293 I'm not one of those people who, by suggesting the
word diversity needs unpacking, would risk making my
white colleagues around the table feel uncomfortable.

294 I'm not one of these people who risks looking directly into the sun.

295 I looked into the microscope and it dawned on me I could now save the lives of millions of people.

296 I opened the box and there was an ant in it.

297 If I hadn't had a call at seven o'clock this morning – which of course turned out to be a wrong number – I might not've been one of those people lucky enough to see the moon's partial eclipse.

298 If my boyfriend hadn't called me back at seven o'clock this morning and – even though I could tell he'd only the dimmest memory of what had actually happened five hours earlier on the fire escape of the Klub Kinshasa – apologised, I might still be one of these people who sees human nature as an electrochemical disaster.

299 If I hadn't had a call at seven o'clock this morning which was from my sister who'd been to our mother's care home and noticed that her wedding ring was missing – and had been incredibly upset all the previous day and been wondering should she call the police? until they'd just phoned her at half past six to say Mum must've taken it off herself because they'd found the ring inside the case of her reading glasses wrapped up in the little polishing cloth – which wasn't of course proof that it hadn't been stolen and then put back, but which nevertheless, so far as my sister was concerned, 'drew a line under it' – which I suppose did explain the seven o'clock phone call, given my sister, a consultant neurologist, is often already at work at that time trying to catch up on the academic articles she writes before she sets off for the

hospital, and might not've had time to call me later,
and anyway thinks that calling people at seven a.m. is
normal – if I hadn't had that call which completely
threw my morning routine – kids out of bed, kids
dressed, kids off to school, radio on, ten minutes to
myself for coffee then out through the door – and
strangely destabilised my mind, making me see our
mother as part of a long animal chain of birth and
death and me and my own children as part of a long
animal chain of birth and death which the wrapped-
up ring in the glasses case seemed to embody, as if we
had no free-will, or let's say, yes, we had free-will, but
the world's will was greater than ours, a blind
overriding force compelling us to love one another
and to reproduce, a force that had no regard for
individual destinies, or the achievements, so-called, of
human culture, seeing no more value in the nine
symphonies of Beethoven or eradication of malaria
than in the successful assembly of a flat-pack coffee
table, neither did that force care (I unwillingly
recognised) about how humans organised their
societies, whether, for example, men valued treating
women equally or on the contrary oppressed and
controlled them, or whether the ruling class embraced
slavery or condemned it as a disgusting crime, it was
all the same to this blind force provided that children
were born and the dead disposed of. Yes if I hadn't
been put by my twin sister's phone call into this odd
state of mind which persisted even as I was making
my own twins their breakfast and shooing them out
of the flat in the matching backpacks they insisted
on – chatting to them all the time in a way which
only seemed to underline how much the life we lead
is mechanical and almost involuntary since the cues
between me and my children are basically automatic
even when it comes to moral questions about stealing
and lying which may on the surface of it seem to

require thought but are in fact almost reflexively answered according to certain principles which we parents unconsciously acquire and equally unconsciously pass on to our children who probably don't even need moral instruction if we are to believe certain geneticists and behavioural scientists who detect a hard-wired propensity towards fairness and redistributive behaviour in children even as young as three. If I hadn't, finally, been so distracted when I myself clicked shut the door behind me as I left for work by a sense that everything that had so far happened and would happen in the future – migration, the rise and fall of empires, new ways to configure the family, new kinds of technology, all truth, all beauty, all puritanical terror and mad party-going – was absolutely predetermined and had little or no connection with what is currently called human agency (and did that make me a potential fascist? or was it more a kind of super-cool Buddhist thing?) I might well've stopped for a moment to think about the weather, in which case I'd've had an umbrella with me and would not've run quite so recklessly back into the building when it began to rain.

On Writing *Not One of These People*

At the beginning of 2020 I began a conversation with Vicky Featherstone, artistic director of London's Royal Court Theatre, about making work that could be performed as soon as the conditions of pandemic 'lockdown' eased and audiences could return. Naively, we assumed it would happen soon.

I wondered what would be the ingredients of such a piece? Firstly, to avoid physical contact between actors and involve little or no rehearsal: a text to be read off the page – possibly 'at sight'. Secondly: a text of long duration – maybe even several hours – so that small audience groups could enter at intervals, sampling the text, as it were, before leaving to let the next group in. This second, 'durational' idea was inspired by the UK company Forced Entertainment whose show *Speak Bitterness* – a long enumeration of confessions – had made an indelible impression on me in the 1990s.

So I quickly came up with a plan to write a text of 1,000 voices, each one different, each one to be read from a script with no preparation.

Why this? Literary antecedents, clearly – like a number of people during the pandemic I reread *The Decameron*, falling back in love with its robust storytelling, while absorbing the usefulness of its strict formal scheme. Then there were some recent encounters I'd had with young dramatists where I'd been struck by their anxiety about who or what they were permitted to write about, about who they could 'give voice' to. As a playwright – whose job, traditionally at least, is to create conflict between invented humans of diverse characters and biographies, and of opposing but equally valid points of view – I believed this anxiety of theirs to be unfounded – but the more I thought about it, the more I felt my response to them had not been adequate. Perhaps then *Not One of These People* is my much-delayed answer to those young people – an improbably extended *esprit de l'escalier* – while at the same time being, in a more Boccaccian mode, what I hope is an entertaining tour of the streets, squares, public gardens and dead-ends of my own imagination.

I never made it to 1,000. August came and the theatres were still closed. Two years later, Vicky was still keen to produce the work, but, like myself, not sure what a *mise en scène* would look like. The Québécois director Christian Lapointe intervened, with a concept brilliantly linking the text to contemporary internet culture. From this new perspective, it was no longer a text of long duration, but a strange kind of ninety-minute monologue, spoken by myself, and linked to a sequence of photographs of people who do not exist.

Each one of these 299 images has been generated by Artificial Intelligence (by a method known as GAN, or generative adversarial network).* At a certain point they come completely to life, my own voice and facial movements mapped onto theirs live as I speak – a technique familiar from the world of 'deepfake' – but unusual for operating here in real time thanks to the extraordinary work of Guillaume Lévesque at o/i Hub numérique.

All plays move by the very nature of theatre in directions the author cannot predict. This one quietly crept up behind me and decided to put me on stage.

M.C.
September 2022

---

* See, for example: thispersondoesnotexist.com